WHISPERS
OF
THE
SOUL

Alexandra Goodwin

DEDICATION

To my husband, Craig Goodwin, for all that you do

CONTENTS

PREFACE

One day I read a headline about an eight-year-old boy who committed suicide because he was bullied at school for no reason. The boy lived in another state, and I knew nothing about him. However, his pain crossed all visible and invisible paths and landed on my keyboard, where I could not continue to write the business letter I had set out to write at work. His image haunted me for days, until I sat down and poured the pain I felt in the form of a poem. Although the poem won't bring him back, it did bring a certain degree of relief and understanding to me, perhaps acceptance.

I began to write. I found that some of the emotional issues I was dealing with at the moment, felt better after they materialized in the form of rhymes and metered lines. Suddenly, I had filled up a spiral notebook. I had enough poems to collect them in a book.

The photographs are all mine, with the exception of two. Some were taken from my own backyard, others are from the Japanese Gardens at the Morikami Museum in Delray Beach, Florida, and others at the Everglades at Loxahatchee Road. They attempt to capture visually what I felt at the time I took them.

This book is a work of love, and as such, I offer it to you, my reader, so you can share in the emotions that bind us in our human experience. You will cry, you will laugh. And then you will heal.

Alexandra Goodwin
Coral Springs, Florida

Alexandra Goodwin

FOR ALL THAT YOU DO

If I told you that I love you
It would probably be dull.
So instead I'll weave a blanket
With your name across the sky.

How do I love thee?
Listening to the rhythm marked by
Your breathing, soft and steady,
Soothing as if saying: "Look!
I'm here, I'm not going anywhere!"

Your bear hands, like leather
Against my petals,
Your nails that you ate for breakfast
And continue to snack on.

Your hair now thinning, and whitening
Too, witness to a thousand seas of
Grief and joy.

Your clean Irish Spring smell
In the morning, and the sweat of a day's work
Show me what you do for me, for all,
To give us the best of the world.

And your quiet escapades into the
Fridge at night? The door opens and
It stays like that for a while.
You scratch your head, still
Looking for the jelly which is right in
front of your eyes.

Those eyes… onyx
Pearls that sparkle a thousand stars,
Penetrate the depths of my heart,
They see what I can't see
And shed light to my blind walk.

And your heart, the best part of you,
Knows no boundaries when
It comes to love; kindness in you is like the air,
Ever present, always there.

You take my hand in yours and
Look at my diamond ring.
You say: "It's too small! Let's get
You a bigger one, one everyone can see!"

But I look at the diamond and
Can only see one thing:
I already have one,
It's you, my diamond is you!

SACRED PLACES

Alexandra Goodwin

UNDER THE MANGO TREE

With a rustle of its leaves
The mango tree speaks
Inviting the birds to build
Under its canopy their nests.

Home, foundation, refuge
Summers bursting with fruit
And shade.

Scampering squirrels hop,
Reach, nibble,
And squeak.

Everybody feasts on the mango tree,
Including me,
Finding respite from all that
Life gives but continues to steal.

And while the garden flutters,
Sun gleams, rain weeps,
Hurricane rages, the mango
Tree stands still.

Feel the energy pulsating
Through, grow quiet within and grasp
There is no escape for the tree.
To be and continue to give
Is all it can do.

Alexandra Goodwin

THE MOUNTAIN WITHIN

The evening is slipping
Under a sullen gray quilt
While she yearns of climbing
Mountains with violets and streams.

Her restless soul on wings sprawled
The ascension begins
Spirit soaring.

Beloved mound where
Lilies abound and
Fox chases deer while
Bear chases man.

Peace and mist swoop down
On her turmoil,
Love unrequited ripping
Her heart.

Clouds struggle for power
What will cleanse her sadness:
Silence, song, or shower?
Below, the stream prancing,
Breeze dancing,
Wind growing,
A shudder.

Wet grass rises toward
The rain, bashful at first
And then the storm.

She squeezes a tear or two
The current of a dam unleashed
A magical place where all
Dreams are and become true
And pain is washed away.

MUSINGS

Alexandra Goodwin

THE ELUSIVE MUSE

Remembering dreams
Was a natural process
Until the writing teacher
Told us to harness
The power of symbols
With pen and cymbals.

So once the muse knew
She had a job,
She sat on her throne
And complained "My head throbs!
I can't think, I can't fly!
Try your best without me
Please try and comply!"

Thus my muse abandoned me
When I needed her most.
Today is Friday
And my brain is toast.
What will I do
If I can't find
The magic of words
In the richness of the night?

For the material is there,
Quiet and concealed
Until the muse makes it revealed,
The beauty and wit
Of the great American novel
That could be, oh, would be?
Written by me.

EULOGY AT MY FUNERAL

What will you say at my funeral?
I imagine you in shock:
"How could this have happened so suddenly,
I'm sorry, I'm in awe!"

I must admit I'm puzzled
That you dared to show up.
You must be morbose or something
'cause you ignored me while alive.

You get up and offer
A big eulogy on my behalf: "She was
Good, sweet, smart and wonderful,
She wouldn't hurt a fly!"

So why is it that you ignored
Me, when I was still alive?
What made you be so distant,
So aloof it made me cry?

As my soul carves out a passage
Into Heaven for its flight
You joke, eat, drink, and whisper
While you gather in my house.

Next day when it's all over,
You will surely forget,
But the ones who truly loved me
In their hearts I will always dwell.

ANOTHER MUSE POEM

If she would let down her hair
That wraps around a bun
It would cascade in spirals
To her waist, all the way from her crown.

Silver strands
Like the white foam
Of a waterfall.

With birdlike steps
She hovers
Just above my head.
Drags a gauzy lace dress
As if she were a ghost.

She loves to surprise me
In the shower, when I can't write.
Unexpected, but always welcome
She drops her treasures on my lap.

She smiles. Her timeless beauty
Shines like the moon.
Her silver aura envelops
Her magic powers like a balloon.

Pearls of wisdom drop like candy
From her mouth into my brain.
Like raindrops I catch them quickly
Lest they flutter away.

When she visits me, I tell her
"Not now! I'm busy!"
But one thing she can't do:
She can't hear!
So she ignores my pleads of
"Later, please!"
And she stays, smiling,
Floating, hovering
Until I give her a voice.

Only then, she leaves
Empty handed from her gift
From Heaven to me.

CITY

Downtown, the city sleeps.
It reeks of rotten fish. We smell
The rot, we turn the block,
Urine wrinkles our nose.

The buses gouge the smog in the
Air, taint it with black fog,
Burnt rubber, gas, the remnants
Of Chinese fried duck and chicken
Wasting in some dirty wok.

Desolation gnaws.

Then ravages the city whole.

GREAT BEGINNINGS

Slim rivers drip down the frosted glass walls. Outside, it's still dark, as the morning yawns through the waning rays of the moon.

Inside, Japanese paper lanterns droop long and sleek from the ceiling panels, scalloping, staggered, flickering an orange glow to the suit wearing CEO who marches in, her black hair trapped in a neat ponytail, a whiff of Chanel No. 5 trailing behind her, stiletto black heels cloppety-clopping music on the tile.

Disheveled, the stench of crumpled sheets still on his frown, a man staggers in, dark lines under his nails, a gray sloppy t-shirt over a pair of white paint stained slacks. He shifts on his feet as he waits in line.

The lure is comfort, soul comfort at all levels. Fresh baked rye and asiago cheese bagels meddle with the dark and bitter aura of freshly brewed coffee.

The beginning of a perfect day…

ONCE UPON A TIME

Alexandra Goodwin

SONNET OF THE BROKEN LAD

The day Charlene got married he went off
To town, he picked a book of poems and read
It like a clown. A lot of people scoffed
As he began to cry and wished her dead

For she had played his soul a trick and left
Him bleeding, wondering how else she could
Get back at him for sounding so bereft
When she had found him with Anouk.

The world is round, the muse reflects, unbound
By its own fury when love deceives an honest heart
And pricks with thorns of rose that scar the ground
As blood leaves trails of evidence apart,

From such beloved memories. They both
Fulfill their destiny of breaking oaths.

Alexandra Goodwin

ONE MORE
VILLANELLE

We have two but he wants one more,
One more ear to hear him snore?
Perhaps one more companion to walk to the shore.

Whatever the reason, he wants it now.
I dread the work, the stress, the "how."
We have two but he wants one more.

To please him is easy because I love him so,
That any request becomes a "no-chore."
Perhaps one more companion to walk to the shore

Is what he needs when he asks
To go to the store, even though
We have two, and he wants one more.

It's true that they give you so much
Unconditional love, and friendship.
Perhaps one more companion to walk to the shore.

In the end, I know I'll succumb,
And I will agree to get a third dog.
We have two but he wants one more,
Perhaps one more companion to walk to the shore.

FOSTER HOME

He was my foster brother,
He got all the attention
While I sat in his shadow,
Waiting.

He never missed a chance
To settle the score: "You are
The outsider, that's my mom
And my dad."

Winona tried. She always smiled.
She went to see Mr. Jenkins
To talk about me. She was lost.
Nothing was enough.

In the end, I sadly realized
My birth mother would not straighten out.
She had missed too many beats.
The music of her life had no melody, only drums.

She would never come back for me.
My real dad was dead.
I had nothing to lose, except
The one opportunity I got to be loved.

Winona came that night.
And went straight to the back,
She closed the blinds then horrified
She saw the trail of blood.

I can hear still her breathing and
Also when it stopped.
Her howl across the silence
Of a winter night that froze.

Her pain pierced my heart and that's
How I know I have one.
I did not mean to hurt her, only
To be her only one.

IMAGINE THE THRILL

Imagine the thrill
He must have felt
When he spotted the land
He always knew had been there.

Between the sky and miles of smooth water
The promontory rises with the birth of a new day,

He smiles at his crew,
He begins to dance,
Christopher Columbus blesses the day
When he valiantly took a chance.

While the nave approaches
The land that he sees,
His apprehension grows
For it is all unknown.

As they come closer
His heart beats much faster:
What ifs pop up
Like bubbles in boiling water.

What he does not imagine
Is that the land is inhabited:
Somebody beat him to
The fifteenth century discovery.

How could he have fathomed
The existence of other people
Who speak as if they sing,
And wear the sun in their skin?

Remembering the instructions
From Queen Isabella,
He takes the flag and pole
And claims ownership for the throne,
As if it was meant to be their own.

Oh, humanity,
Or lack of it!
Why couldn't we share,
Respect them, step back?

Massacred people who
Knew about the sun
Laugh from their graves now,
And watch down from the stars.

BRAVURA

Despite the tourists yelling
All mothers begging, he
Plunged in the water and swam to the deep.
The ocean is sneakily calling him in.

As people scream and gesture,
He challenges his bravura,
Or is it arrogance?
"He could be depressed,"
Some of them venture.

"Maybe he wants to commit suicide?"
First white then crimson red,
Frantic gulps of lacey foam,
While people grow quiet, but he

Can be heard from the shore,
His arms flailing and bobbing above
The indigo blue of the sinister sea,
Nightmarish slow motion, drowning his plea.

The lifeguard blows his whistle
But doesn't venture in, why should he?
Instead they all stand still
Hoping the mauler will release the kill.

Ruby and silence
That's all there is.
As the great white shark
Gracefully away swims.

BEWILDERED
Dedicated to all victims of bullying

As I walk down the hall this morning
They look at me with mocking eyes.
Others turn away and leave an
Empty space, too big for me alone to pass.

It happened in another school.
What is it that I have?
They hate me and don't speak to me
And surely, I don't know why.

Breathe in. Look around.
I am so alone and sad.
They hate me, that is clear,
And I do not know why.

DUSK

They sit holding hands, just
Like two lovers. Glowing sparks of
Golden red cross the sky as
A mockingbird scouts
The distance, perched
On the fence.

Dusk. Like their years waning by.
She with her white hair, all wrapped in a bun.
He with a cane, to help him get by.

Crossing the air, piercing the sky, a baseball lands
By their feet nearby.

A crystal rain of
Shattering glass
Breaks
The silence in
A thousand shards

As the couple watch, still holding hands.

I WONDER IF IT WAS YOU
A Pantoum

When I turned on the TV this morning
I tuned in to the news.
A hiker's body was found dead
And I wondered if it was you.

I tuned in to the news this morning
The Grand Canyon was his grave
I wondered if the found body
Could have possibly belonged to you.

The Grand Canyon is the grave
Of a stubborn, selfish, male.
Could it possibly have been you
The hiker nobody knew?

If a stubborn, selfish, male
Whose body ended up on the trail
A hiker nobody knew
Except me, when I tuned on the news.

Whose body was found dead?
A hiker's body on a trail.
Could it possibly have been you?
I wonder as I watch the news.

Alexandra Goodwin

THREE SISTERS

Up in the moors, under the clouds
Sturdy and wide there is a stone house,
Stretching upward, brown and cold,
Mysteriously enveloped in its own shroud.

From the valley below, nothing is known,
Except for the icy ominous walls
That trap ancient stories written by all
Talented sisters wrapped in their shawls.

During the day there is no sign
Of life. But at night the stone house
Becomes mystically alive,
As three shadows parade in the candlelight.

As in a trance they furiously write
Till the break of dawn all through the night,
Those words that death stole from them
Despite their lonely plight.

Three women living in the sturdy stone house.
Sisters that unflinching, refuse to die.
They whisper their words to poets alive,
The Brontes, Emily, Charlotte, and Anne.

HEALING

Alexandra Goodwin

BRIDGES

I'd like to write a poem
to try to understand
My feelings when my anger
Emerges and expands.

Why weren't we invited
To the wedding of Darlene?
While all of them are dancing
We wonder and stay in.

We've known them for twelve years,
Belonged to the same group.
They played dumb when they sadly,
Our name chose to maroon.

Let's step back for a moment,
And give it a hard look
As we begin to question
The validity of the lessons we took.

What if Goths and Christians,
And Muslims, Blacks, and Jews,
Decided to come together
And sing in tune the Blues?

Would that spark soulful fires,
And build a bridge of love
And let us feel the power
Of the world in our hands?

Because we've been indoctrinated
To only love our own,
It's when they don't love you back
You realize you don't belong.

WAKE UP CALL

As you wake up one morning,
You stretch, and shed back
The blanket that warmed you
All night. Your safety.

Yawning, you open up like
A flower, and then venture
Onto the cold floor.
A gray day. No sun.

Thrust in the whirlwind of work, chores,
Or just existing, there is no
Going back. Like on a belt
From an assembly line, you
Must move, always looking forward,
Never looking back.

YOGA CLASS

We start by closing our eyes.
The lights are dimmed.
In the quiet darkness,
I begin to breathe.

Air going in, through the nose,
Pause, hold, push away that thought,
Exhale long and deep,
And repeat.

The present moment, like a single point
On a blank page.
Nothing before it, or in front.
Pure now and bliss.

The intensity of nothingness
Overwhelms me.
Peace surrounds me while
My breath slow dances with my heart.

Stretch, and touch
Your toes with your fingers.
Breathe in, hold, breathe out.
And again.

Awareness of something
Running through my spine.
It's my cells, suddenly alive.

On my feet now, I bend forward,
Making a triangle with
My body. Every muscle
Fiber pulls and lengthens,
A vision of a chrysanthemum
Breaking free from its bud.

Pull forward: the plank.
Hold parallel to the ground.
Feel the connection with
Everything that is.
And breathe.

Go down, chin touching chest,
Stretch your arms:
Cobra. Tuck in your feet,
Pull yourself up, and down
In downward facing dog.
Five times.

Heart racing now, muscles elasticized
Tested to the limit, skin moist,
Trying to control the breath.

Lie down on your back.
Eyes closed.
Let go. Surrender.
And breathe.

ZEN

Imagined, but unseen,
Conceived and dreamed,
Desired, craved for, anticipated,
Longed for,
Tomorrow.

Tasted, sensed, touched,
Endured, encountered,
Lived to the fullest, perhaps.
Regretted, is more likely.
Yesterday.

Tangible, palpable,
Resplendent, manifest,
Attainable,
In your face.
Today.

Is what counts.

WORKING IT OUT

You can't hold the burden
That weighs down your heart.
Your disappointment hides
Behind your faint smile.

You look around
And all you see
Is the failure you achieved.
You worked in vain and
Nothing matters anymore.

As your mind escapes
To where it can disconnect
It begins to repair the
Path for success.

Close your eyes and
You will see cream
Sandy beaches, a
Cool green blue sea.

Immerse in the water,
Come out refreshed, the
Salt of your tears will
Sway your love to emerge.

Take a deep breath and
Swallow your pride; ask
Him for a hug,
Then sigh
When all the passion of his love

Alexandra Goodwin

Will embrace
You
In his
Arms.

THE GIFT

Thoughts of wonder as I ponder
On life as a gift from yonder.
I immerse in a world of bliss.

Another day.

A gift.

ACCESS DENIED

I've been knocking on this door
For such a long time now,
As others go in
I am left to wonder,
Why is access to me denied?

As they pass me by, they smile,
They do, never forgetting their manners
But as I try to get in,
Access to me is denied.

I hear laughter from the inside.
It's cold outside.
I wait and I wonder,
Why is access to me denied?

Dusk drops a gray
Blanket heavy on the night.
Light through the window
Oozes friendship and love.
But access to me is denied.

Night closes in. Orion readies its bow
For the fight. I leave this place forever,
Where I sat for so long
Knocking on the same door
While access to me was always denied.

Encouraged by the stars
That embroider with diamonds the sky
I venture out.

My journey begins now.
It's cold outside.

Although my steps only the owls can hear,
The dry soil crunches under my fear.
I follow the stars and immerse in the night
For the sun tomorrow will appear.

And then I will have survived the night,
The silence, the cold, and the dark,
Even though access
To me
Was denied.

RECOVERY

The time to get up and
Embark on the journey of discovery
Came one day unexpected
When I realized I needed recovery.

It's been an addiction,
A true contradiction
To grasp and hold on to
Situations that cause friction.

Tears, like raindrops,
Fall and form a puddle
Dislodging my prison,
Launching my struggle.

More like an uphill climb during
Winter in Nepal
It sums up your strength, your core,
If you give it your all.

But even if you don't reach
The Summit, you will have learned
That every step you take
Along the way, carves a little piece of the top.

I did it, with help.
You can too.
Good for you,
And for me.

GAMES AND SPONGE CAKE

Tuesday afternoon.

Down the long dark corridor,
Our steps resonate with eco.
Grandma's apartment, my refuge.

Knock-knock "Who's there?"
The game begins. "It's the fairy!"
"A fairy! Oh my!" The door opens,
Giggles begin.

The smell of sponge cake
Baking in the oven,
Sugar and vanilla, hot chocolate
Too. I know the routine.

I go to her bedroom, open the closet,
Take off my shoes,
Put on her black, low heel pumps,
And flip-flop back to the living room.

She's already bringing the tray
With the spongy, vanilla smell
Of her cake arranged in slices,
Like dominoes after the game.

She sets it on the table, and brings
A mug with milk. Steam rises
From the bittersweet chocolate.
"Let the party begin!"

The tablecloth is sprinkled with
Forget-me-nots and leaves.
Lilac, green, and yellow too
Smile and greet me with glee.

She puts a linen napkin on
my lap, the lacy edges crocheted
By hand. Beige on white, subtle
And refined.

As we pretend to play "guests"
She inquires after my life.
"What have you been up to, dear?"
"Oh, all kinds of nifty things…!"

I learn about manners, watching
Her eat the cake, and lifting
Her cup so delicately, I try
To do the same.

When it's time to leave her,
She wraps me in her shawl.
"It's cold outside, my darling,"
"I know, Grandma, I know."

I take with me the most beautiful
Treasure of all: a dose of love
And comfort that will carry me
Till next Tuesday.

Every week, rain or shine,
Winter, summer, we visit,
But today, the hall is dark,

Our steps heavy, no games behind
The door.

The kitchen is wrapped in
Bleach, and her shoes are gone.

STAND NAKED UNDER THE RAIN

Raw, present, full of dread,
Your fears laid out like a
Mantle of lead.
Your earnest desires demand
Satisfaction
Right now, immediate,
Without hesitation.

What lies in the deepest
Cave of your heart
All of a sudden emerges
Like a butterfly,
Timid and shy,
As you fall in love
With the freedom the words
Your poetry provides.

Stand naked under the rain!
Freeze your pain.
Needles of water
Will pierce your face,
And paint it with tears
Of pure happiness.

TWO STICKS IN A BUN

She carries her belly like a cinnamon
Bun, brown and oozing sweetness
Despite her bitter past.
Her legs are two sticks,
Leathered and worn out.

Silently howling her journeys untold,
Her innermost peace is seemingly lost.
Straw on her head still grimy
From the shelter's soap,
She smiles at me anyway, as I approach.

"Lovely morning!" she chimes nonchalant.
Now, why would she say that?
I look up and see in her sad eyes
A yearning to connect to something mighty grand.

Someone in a Lexus honks, impatient,
So she turns around and
Hops to the car diligently,
A newspaper in her left hand.

Two sticks in a bun is thus jolted
back to her meager life.
I look down, ashamed of my luck,
While I quietly hurry past.

The message is so simple
and yet so exceedingly vast,
How much love and healing can be held
in one beautiful smile.

So I dazzle mine, as I walk by.
"May you be blessed!" she chirps again.
You may think I must have made her day.

But here is the secret:
She is the one
Who has
Made mine.

HAIKU

句集

Alexandra Goodwin

Sand on the beach

Eighty five thousand grains in

One millimeter.

Zucchini blooms bright

Under a fiery sun

Crawls and stretches wide.

Sand, rocks, and water,

Blue salt, sun high in the sky,

The Universe sings.

Red robin flies low,

Seeds in her beak then to nest,

Motherly instinct.

Haiku exists

For the sake of brevity,

The here and now.

Alexandra Goodwin

In her green blanket

She peeks through

Seeking the sun.

Full moon rising

Like a bubble

From the sea.

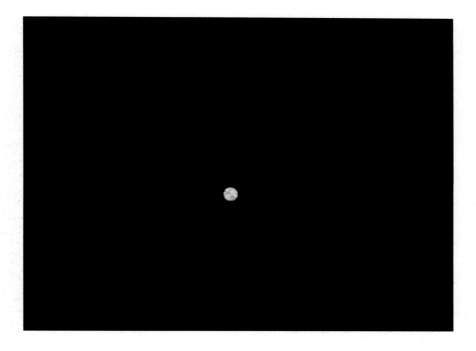

Like a falling star

A blue jay flies from the nest.

Perches on the fence.

Tosses in the breeze,

Smiles and dances like a queen.

She owns the garden.

Otherwise peaceful,

In the distance, a crow

Breeze in the sawgrass

What a thousand words

Cannot say, an image can:

Promise in a bud.

Like the orange tree

Blooms in Florida's winter,

I thrive in the cold.

Meditate, think now,

Be still in the silence of

What surrounds you.

Alexandra Goodwin

The sun is setting,

Stillness descends from Heaven,

The Sabbath begins.

Water falling down

A rock into a pool,

Crystal and light

A moment to feel

My solitude, the quiet,

Much needed relief.

One haiku a day,

And watch your soul aligning

With the Universe...

Alexandra Goodwin

ABOUT THE AUTHOR

Alexandra Goodwin was born in Buenos Aires, Argentina, and came to the United States as a student. After raising two wonderful children with her husband, and despite her full time job as a bookkeeper, one day she packed up her lifelong excuses, locked them up in the attic, and sat down to write under her mango tree. Surrounded by blue jays and red robins that come to fill their nests every spring, she escapes the Florida heat by immersing herself in the cool waters of her imagination, and creates worlds she hopes to share with her readers as they come to life. She lives with her husband Craig and their two white poodles in Coral Springs, Florida. This is her first book of poetry. Visit her website at www.alexandragoodwin.com.

Made in the USA
Columbia, SC
16 August 2019